The Poetry of IKEBANA

The Poetry of
IKEBANA

Noriko Ohno
KOKUSAI IKEBANA ASSOCIATION

KODANSHA INTERNATIONAL
Tokyo and New York

Distributed in the United States by Kodansha International/USA Ltd.,
114 Fifth Avenue, New York, New York 10011. Published by Kodansha International Ltd., 17-14, Otowa 1-chome, Bunkyo-ku, Tokyo 112
and Kodansha International/USA. Copyright © 1990 by Kodansha International Ltd. All rights reserved. Printed in Japan.

ISBN 4-7700-1467-8 (Japan)
ISBN 0-87011-967-2 (U.S.)

Library of Congress Cataloging-in-Publication Data

Ōno, Noriko.
    The poetry of Ikebana / Noriko Ohno.
      p.   cm.
    1. Flower arrangement, Japanese. I. Title.
SB450.0494 1990
745.92'252—dc20   90-40221

CONTENTS

FOREWORD

The world is full of beautiful flowers. People everywhere arrange flowers for all kinds of occasions and events in their daily lives. Like poetry, flower arrangement can be formal or informal, happy or sad, serious or spontaneous. It is simply a part of human nature, one of many ways to celebrate events or to express emotions.

The Japanese art of flower arrangement, ikebana, originated on this natural principle. But over the centuries, different styles of ikebana developed into warring schools, which managed to make the art inaccessible to all but the most committed students. As ikebana began to be introduced overseas, it was presented not as a living part of Japanese culture but rather as a difficult and codified art form full of rigid, intimidating rules.

I established the Kokusai ("International") Ikebana Association in 1955 with the hope of dispelling that image and opening up the world of ikebana to all people who love flowers. Also, I was certain that fresh input from abroad would revitalize ikebana, surpassing the bounds of each school and developing a world-encompassing art form that would respect individuality and embrace modernity. In this way, I believed, ikebana would not only be an element of, but an active participant in, international cultural communication.

Since then, my belief that ikebana itself is international, and not limited to any particular method, continues to deepen through the many international friendships I have developed. Though highly ornamental Western floral art uses blossoms as design material only, the Japanese attitude toward floral arrangement is a deeper, more spiritual one. The two most important philosophies of ikebana—that the arrangement must fit the environment in which it is displayed and that the individual arranger's emotions and character are to be expressed in the arrangement—are precisely what make ikebana in its ideal state perfectly adaptable to all kinds of countries, all kinds of flowers, and especially all kinds of people.

Constant interaction between Japanese and non-Japanese arrangers has resulted in a very free form of ikebana that incorporates the color schemes, flowers, and vases of all countries. I have included basic instructions in the back of this book which present the standard styles and techniques taught in ikebana, but you will see from the photographs of my creations that I encourage all kinds of variations—even humorous ones. I have chosen to show most of my arrangements with blank backgrounds in order to emphasize the flowers and containers used, but I hope that your ikebana arrangements will involve more than just containers and flowers but also, perhaps, large spaces, music, and overall design elements; please use your own imagination and my hints in the captions to determine a good setting for each arrangement.

In keeping with the international theme, I have identified the country where I found each vase and, in fact, shown that some of the vases are ones that I made myself, primarily on a trip to the island of Majorca, off the coast of Spain. Also, since ikebana emphasizes individual creativity and emotions, I have included a section on personal impressions of people and events that shows best what I mean by ikebana being an art of human communication. You will find, as I have, that a floral portrait of a friend or loved one is a gift that will be appreciated for long after the flowers are gone.

I hope you will enjoy this book and use it whenever you need hints for your own arrangements.

THE HISTORY OF IKEBANA

Ikebana has a long history. The famous eleventh-century miscellany "Makura no Soshi" (*The Pillow Book*) mentions "Cherry blossoms in a celadon vase," and the diaries of the Kamakura period (1185–1333) speak of flowers arranged for Tanabata, the July festival of the stars. The formal art of ikebana, however, traditionally dates from the Muromachi period (1392–1568). This was an age most famous for the widespread wrangling among the feudal lords of the nation and the warfare that left Kyoto, the seat of most of the country's culture, in ashes. But it was also an age when lively and exciting new art forms developed. Ikebana, one of those new developments, ceased being merely a way of arranging floral offerings (*kuge*) to the Buddha and began to crystallize as an art form appreciated for itself. *Tatebana* ("standing flowers") became a fashionable elaborate flower arrangement style—better known by the name of *rikka*—that shared the seat of honor with a special brand of *tatebana* simultaneously developing in the Imperial Court.

At that time, townspeople were rapidly growing financially powerful, and so they began to put on exhibitions rivaling those of the court nobles. These exhibitions gradually grew into formal associations, the forebears of the now-famous ikebana schools. As ikebana grew into a full-fledged art, attention began to shift from the flowers to the arrangers themselves. Then, as the *rikka* style grew more and more elaborate, the tea ceremony came into fashion. The flowery majesties of the *rikka* were completely unsuitable for the Zen-inspired tea drinking practices. Another style was needed, and the tea masters invented it themselves: the charming and simple style called *nageire* (literally "tossed in"), also known as *chabana,* or tea flowers.

Nageire is characterized by the aesthetic of a single blossom and a single leaf. The main aim of these simple arrangements was to recreate the natural look of flowers growing in the field. The soft and refined tastes of the tea ceremony gained in popularity and with them so did the *nageire* style, which soon demanded simple, rough vases of exquisite coloration to replace the painted porcelain affairs previously in mode. Baskets made of bamboo and fitted with containers for water made superb tea-ceremony flower containers, as we can tell from the famous flower basket now kept in Onjō-ji temple and attributed to the most famous of all the tea masters, Sen no Rikyū.

Gradually, ikebana developed into an ornamental and artistic form so deeply infused with the typical Japanese love of beauty and nature that flower arranging has become not just an art form but more a philosophy, an aesthetic, much treasured by the Japanese people.

The Poetry of IKEBANA

Each of the arrangements on the following pages is supplemented by a line drawing showing the basic structure of the arrangement, and the relative positions of the chief branches. A large circle denotes the first chief branch; smaller circles represent the second and third. For general information on chief branches, please see page 99.

Spring

Serenity

MATERIALS: Canary Island Date Palm bud
CONTAINER: Stone urn (France)

We must be able to step away from our daily concerns and look calmly at the world around us in order to really understand our purpose in life. The moment that one accepts one's existence is also the moment that one realizes one must help others. This is true serenity.

When I first glimpsed this 300-year-old stone jug in the country in France, something stirred in my chest and I was filled with contentment. Entrusting my dreams to the young palm bud, I composed this arrangement to express a perfectly serene heart.

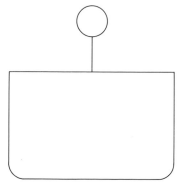

Happy New Year

MATERIALS: Pine, Bamboo, Weeping Willow
CONTAINER: Ceramic ware (Nice)

Pine for long life, bamboo to drive away adversity, willow for natural greenness—these are the materials used in arrangements to celebrate the New Year in Japan.

NOTE: Arrange the pine and the bamboo in the container first, and finish by shaping the willow into a ring for a quiet, composed effect.

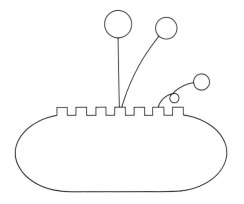

Floral Message

MATERIALS: Snow Camellia
CONTAINER: Made by the author (Majorca)

The fully bloomed camellias in the two openings balance with the half-opened blossom on the water at the center. The flower, without any leaves, floats as if in some fantastic world of dreams.

NOTE: The flowers have been cut very short, so they will last long.

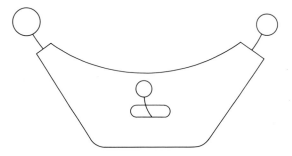

Dancing Ballerinas

MATERIALS: Camellia, Balloon Vine
CONTAINER: Glassware (Okinawa)

Watching the red camellias bloom takes me back to when
I was a little girl and gathered camellias to thread into a
necklace.

The delicate balloon vine twined around the graceful
camellias expresses the dance of a ballerina.

NOTE: For a different effect, any one of the vases in this trio of arrangements may stand alone, retaining its lovely dancing lines. The
simplicity of the single flower in each vase is reminiscent of the *nageire*
arrangements used in Japanese tea ceremonies.

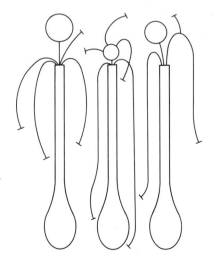

Dancing Flowers

MATERIALS: Anthurium, two varieties of Statice, Carnation, Weeping Willow
CONTAINER: Crystal vase (Sasaki Glass, Japan)

The flowing lines of the weeping willow express a fluid dance, different from that of the dainty ballerinas on the previous page. This arrangement suits a western-style room, and can be viewed from any angle.

NOTE: Add the weeping willow last like a decorative sprinkle. Use gentle lines to create movement.

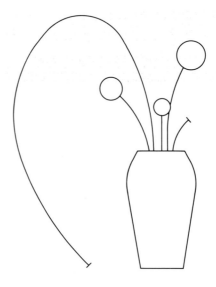

Hearth and Home

MATERIALS: Rape Blossom, Pansy, Sweet Pea, Calla,
Spirea, Rose, Gloriosa, Mimosa, Poppy, Oncidium,
Stock, wine bottles
CONTAINER: Cauldron (Spain)

The fire burns warm. Though it may be cold outside,
spring is here. Colorful flowers gather together like
fairies. Let's open the wine. The party is about to begin.

Ikebana arrangements are not oil paintings or museum
pieces. Since they're an expression of life, why shouldn't
they be touched? The wine bottles in this arrangement
are meant to be opened and enjoyed, not just viewed
from a distance. As the bottles are taken out one by one,
the flowers shift and make new arrangements for your
guests to enjoy.

NOTE: This kind of happy corner brightens any room and makes a
perfect festive addition to the decor. The tree materials extend out-
wards, while the flowers sit prettily at the center.

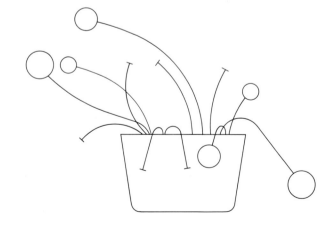

Spring Has Come

MATERIALS: Tulip (pink), Monstera, *Allium schubertii*,
   glass tube
CONTAINER: Pink Glassware (France)

Spring is in the air and everything is suddenly bright and
bursting with life. The colors of the materials and the container are subdued and warm, while the dried *Allium
schubertii* gives the arrangement a sense of exploding
new growth.

NOTE: Dried and fresh flowers of the same species can create very different effects. See "Deep Sea," p. 45, for an example of fresh *Allium
schubertii*.

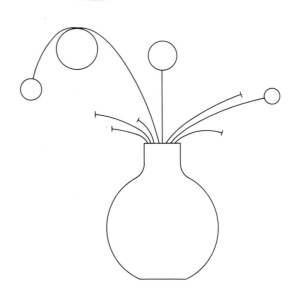

Get-Together

MATERIALS: Spirea, Mimosa, Gladiolus
CONTAINER: White earthenware

I created this arrangement with a merry spring get-together in mind. When placed on a table, it makes a lovely centerpiece that is attractive from all directions. These spring flowers in soft, sunny tones warm the heart and inspire pleasant conversation.

NOTE: Keep the arrangement low so that it does not obstruct the view of the diners, and choose flowers whose fragrance will not interfere with the aroma of the dishes. You may also think about coordinating the colors with the table-cloth and napkins, and scattering lemons and glass balls around the arrangement to enhance the bright atmosphere. The natural asymmetry is set off best when the arrangement is placed diagonally across the table.

Joy

MATERIALS: Sweet Pea (red), Stock (white), White
   Trumpet Lily, Calla (white), Bleached Statice
   (*Limonium latifolia*)
CONTAINER: Red glassware (Finland)

Red and white express vibrant joy and welcome for the
new season after the long winter. The brightly colored
vase emphasizes the festive mood of the flowers.

NOTE: This arrangement is actually two arrangements in one. The container holds two complete sets of branch groups, one on the left and the other on the right. For an explanation of branch groups and arrangement styles, see the "Basic Instructions" section in the back of this book.

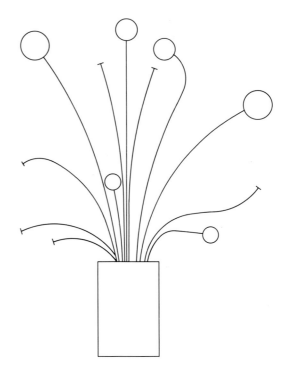

Spring Sea

MATERIALS: Japanese Quince, Sea Fan
CONTAINER: Handmade pots (New Zealand)

Leisurely and carefree, the spring sea extends to the horizon. This arrangement expresses the calm, glorious spring sea, covered with a light haze.

NOTE: This arrangement is another combination of two arrangements, this time in separate containers.

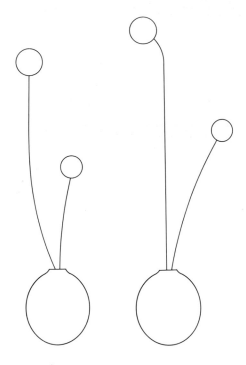

Glass Fantasy

MATERIALS: Showy Lily, Smilax, White Lace Flower,
   Corn Lily (Ixia), glass flower, glass rods
CONTAINER: Glassware (Sasaki Glass, Japan)

The combination of the glass flower, the bulbous glass
rods, and the fresh flowers creates a world of whimsy.
The atmosphere is heightened by the dreamy, romantic
white lace flower.

NOTE: Artificial materials can add a new flavor to your arrangements.
In this case, the glass flower, rods, and vase are all made of frosted
glass, which binds them to each other and creates a unified look. The
fresh lily and the glass flower harmonize beautifully also, and their
bond brings the natural and artificial materials together.

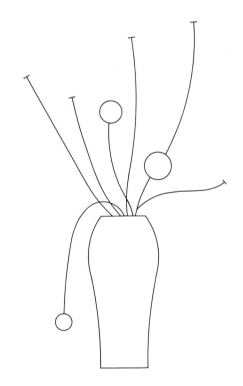

Wind of Joy

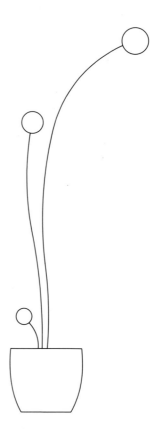

MATERIALS: Anthurium (pink), New Zealand Flax, Cottonweed, Ivory Thistle
CONTAINER: Stoneware (Vietnam)

Subdued colors suggest a gentle spring zephyr. The combination of fresh and dried materials expresses my image of spring and the resurgence of life.

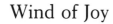

Dream World

MATERIALS: Star-of-Bethlehem, Belladonna Lily, nylon
 net
CONTAINER: Made by the author (Majorca)

I found this soft net-like nylon wrapping material in the corner of a flower market in Denmark. It is used to wrap fruit or flowers gently. I thought these discarded wrapping materials were really beautiful, and I brought some back to use in my arrangements. The bright color seems to be emanating from the soft, romantic material, creating an atmosphere of fantasy.

NOTE: It is important to become aware of the beauty surrounding you in your daily life, and use it creatively. Beauty is everywhere, and we should always be prepared to find it in the most unlikely of places.

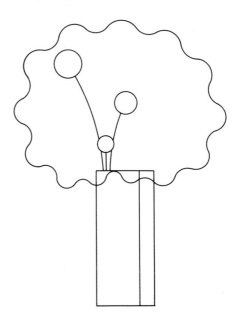

Waltz

MATERIALS: Weeping Willow, Tree Peony (pink)
CONTAINER: Basket

This arrangement expresses quiet stillness at the heart of movement. The large-flowered peony appears to be dancing a floral waltz along the beautiful lines suggested by the weeping willow.

NOTE: Tea rooms used for Japanese formal tea ceremonies always contain a *tokonoma* alcove in which to display an ikebana arrangement suited to the mood of the ceremony. I have always been impressed by hanging style arrangements used in the tea ceremony, in which the container is attached to the wall of the alcove. This arrangement is my expression of the emotion that those arrangements stir in me. Although it uses materials and a container that are often used in the *tokonoma*, it is displayed on a modern concrete wall, bringing Japanese tradition into a new light.

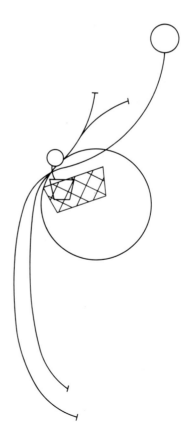

Summer

Movement and Stillness

MATERIALS: Herbaceous Peony, Japanese Bulrush
CONTAINER: White earthenware

The slightest variation can make a single flower and a single stem express opposite ideas. The single Japanese bulrush laid horizontally expresses calm stillness. When the stem is bent upward, suddenly there is an impression of dramatic movement.

NOTE: The arrangement in "stillness" can be viewed from all four directions when placed on a table.

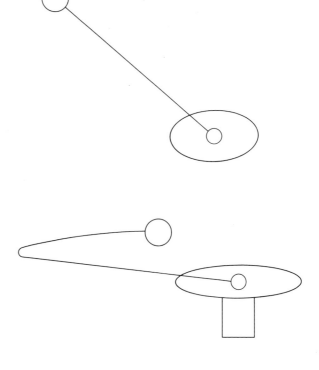

The Forest Blacksmith

MATERIALS: Ananas Flower, Bells-of-Ireland
CONTAINER: Glassware (Aji Rousseau, France)

Flower arrangements need sound, like the rhythms and
melodies that echo inside our minds. This glassware
seemed to call out for a humorous expression of the echo-
ing sound of the blacksmith in the forest.

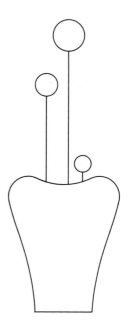

Deep Sea

MATERIALS: *Allium schubertii*, Casablanca Lily, Lemon, crystal ball, seashell
CONTAINER: Transparent spherical glassware (Italy)

This is an underwater scene in August. The fragrant lily, lemons, and seashells—with their secret sound of the waves—remind me of Baudelaire's words that poetry should have smell, color, and sound.

NOTE: When you arrange flowers in transparent glassware, it is important to pay attention to the arrangement inside the container as well as the one outside. The light reflects on the lemons, seashells, and crystal balls in the container, creating a new beauty.

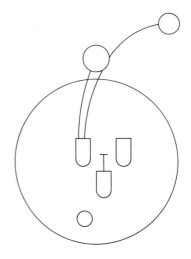

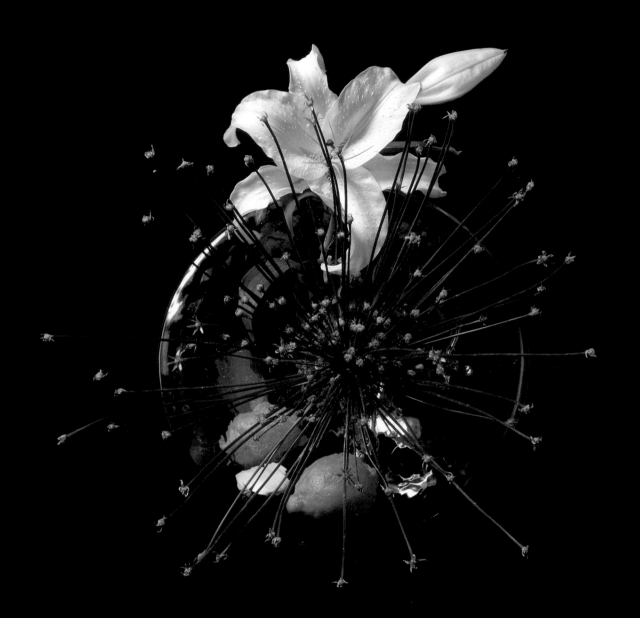

Whispering Summer Fairy

MATERIALS: Lily, Teasel
CONTAINER: Blue glassware (Italy)

The scent of this large, fragrant lily takes your breath away. The whisper of summer seems to tug at your heart.

NOTE: The simple lines and delicate materials arranged in the translucent container give this arrangement a sense of coolness that is always welcome in the summer months.

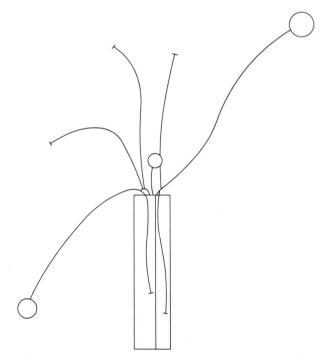

Floral Communication

MATERIALS: Prairie Gentian, Fatsia Japonica
CONTAINER: Transparent spherical glassware (Italy)

These youthful summer leaves seem to be having a conversation. I wonder what they are talking about.

NOTE: This spherical container has three openings for stems. The black pebbles inside the container stabilize the arrangement.

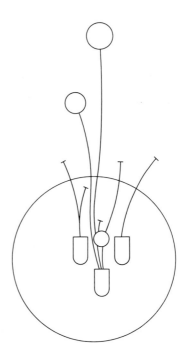

Whirlpool

MATERIALS: Golden Calla, Tree Fern shoot, glass ring
(home-made)
CONTAINER: Glassware (Rosenthal, West Germany)

The glass ring, the curled-up fern, and the spherical container suggest whirling water.

NOTE: For the flower under water, fill the container half-full of water, and float the flower. Here, too, pay attention to the appearance of the arrangement inside the container.

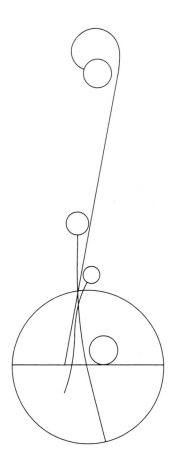

Fall

Autumn Festival

MATERIALS: Lily, Stock, Yam (bleached), Palm (dried),
   chinaware
CONTAINER: Flower vase (Denmark)

This is my impression of a Japanese autumn festival
parade when young people march down the street with
colorful portable shrines on their shoulders. It resounds
with the happy voices of the villagers.

NOTE: The chinaware objets from the South of France have been attached to thick wires, and the single lily with the same vivid hue peeps
out from among the dried palm to celebrate the autumn festival. There
is a clear sense of movement.

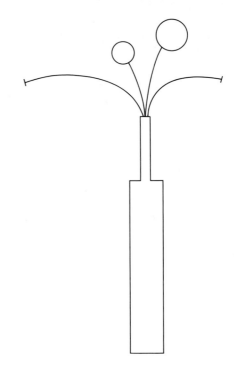

Hope

MATERIALS: White Camellia, Pine, Weeping Willow,
Cucumber Vine
CONTAINER: Bizen earthenware (Japan, Edo period,
ca. 1890)

When guests come for special occasions such as New
Year or a seasonal celebration, a dignified arrangement is
called for. Traditional Japanese flowers are arranged in an
old Japanese pot; yet this is a distinctly modern and
creative arrangement.

NOTE: A tree stump is placed in the opening of the Bizen earthenware
to show off the rings. There is a hole in the center with a cylinder in
which to put the water.
  If you put salt in the flowers, the camellias last longer. Wipe the
camellia leaves clean to keep them beautifully glossy.

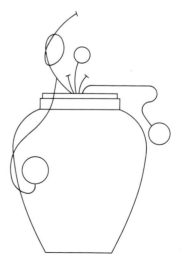

Autumn Harmony

MATERIALS: Balloon Milkweed, Castor Oil Plant
CONTAINER: Made by the author (Majorca)

The colors and shapes of the materials and the container blend in a unique harmony particularly suited to the colors of autumn. Using containers I made myself always allows me to express my personality in original ways.

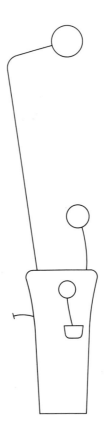

September Song

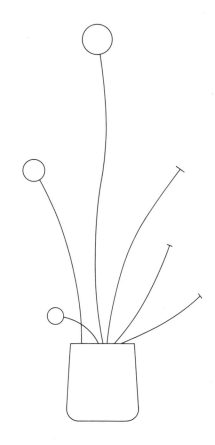

MATERIALS: Prairie Gentian, Patrinia, Chinese Lantern
Plant, Chinese Miscanthus, Arabian Star-of-
Bethlehem, flower made of bamboo (from Estonia,
U.S.S.R.)
CONTAINER: Basket designed by the author (the opening is
left unwoven)

The stalks of unwoven bamboo are arranged with the
flowers, forming a melange of flowers and container. I
have tried to take advantage of the interesting contrast between the fresh and dried materials.

Can you hear the melody from "September Song"?

NOTE: The bamboo folk-craft flower, which I found on an exhibition
tour in Estonia, fits nicely with the bamboo basket and adds an interesting touch to the entire arrangement.

Humorous Face

MATERIALS: Fox Face, Balloon Milkweed
CONTAINER: Unglazed earthenware (Japan)

The unique shapes of the fox face and balloon milkweed combine to make an almost clownish face. This kind of flower arrangement, placed in the corner of a room, helps people to relax, and makes first-time guests feel at home.

NOTE: Although there are only three branches, this is another example of two arrangements placed in one container.

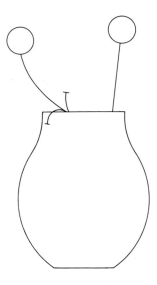

Floral Orchestra

MATERIALS: White Camellia, Oriental Bittersweet
CONTAINER: Woven bamboo

The melody emanating from a single flower expands to form an orchestra of flowers. The floral orchestra echoes in the limpid air as autumn turns into winter.

NOTE: Unlike an ordinary basket, this bamboo container can be stood up or laid down to make entirely different types of containers. Place a neutral-colored vase with water inside the woven container, and thread the camellias through the bamboo weave—or let them peek out from the side.

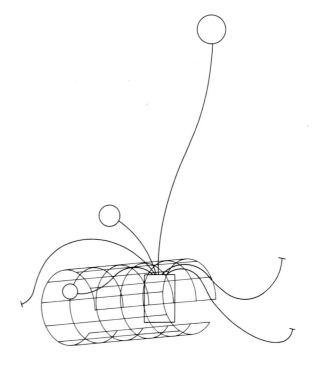

High Spirits

MATERIALS: Gloriosa
CONTAINER: Made by the author (Majorca)

A simple happiness is expressed through the rhythmical arrangement of a single variety of flower. This gloriosa displays the distinctive colors of autumn, and brings out the warm colors in the multi-colored vase.

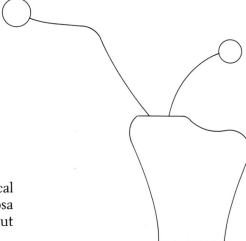

Harvest

MATERIALS: Orange, Chrysanthemum
CONTAINER: Made by the author (Majorca)

When the green oranges begin to take on a yellow hue,
the harvest season is on its way. The miniature chrysan-
themums with green centers express a joyful welcome for
the autumn harvest.

NOTE: For this type of arrangement, set up the orange branches first
to establish the basic form.

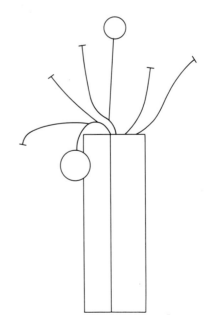

Song of Autumn

MATERIALS: Fox Face, Painted Maple, Japanese Stewartia, Solidaster Luteus

CONTAINER: A pair of vases (South of France)

When autumn is full upon us, the trees come aflame with bright crimson and yellow leaves. The fox face and solidaster are arranged in the center for a joyful song.

NOTE: Autumn leaves that have changed color can fall off easily. If you spray a sugar solution to secure them and add gloss, the arrangement will last longer.

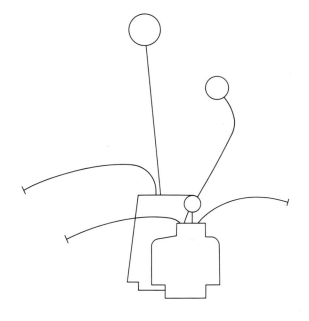

Winter

Excitement

MATERIALS: Carnation, Japanese Catalpa
CONTAINER: Handmade earthenware (Spain)

The brilliant carnation at the focus of the dried materials is a startling expression of the sense of excitement.

The muted colors of the dried materials and the container make the carnation stand out, and the lines of the bent catalpa echo the lines etched into the container, acting to extend the container into the space around it.

Stately Dance

MATERIALS: King Protea, Japanese Catalpa
CONTAINER: Made by the author

Australia has many varieties of unusual flowers, and the king protea is certainly no exception. Here is another use of the catalpa I used in "Excitement" (p. 71)—this time expressing the horizontal rather than the vertical.

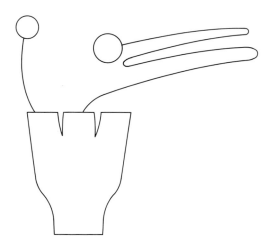

Merry Christmas

MATERIALS: Anthurium, Monstera, White Lace Flower,
  glass tube, Christmas ornaments, cotton
CONTAINER: Glassware (Sasaki Glass, Japan)

The red, white, and green colors evoke the joyful spirit of
Christmas. The delicate white lace flower suggests the
falling snow, which—together with Christmas decora-
tions such as reindeer and a candy cane—conjures up the
airy atmosphere of a horse-drawn sleigh coursing through
the snow.

NOTE: Since the anthurium flower is particularly large and flat, slight
variations in its position and angle will have a pronounced effect on the
whole arrangement. Use anthurium of different sizes and colors (red,
pale red, and green) to advantage.

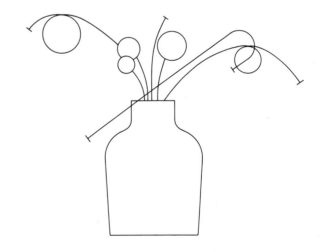

Impressions

Napoleon

MATERIALS: Anthurium, Belvedere, *Alpinia kumatake* berries
CONTAINER: Earthenware shaped like Napoleon's hat (Masuo Ikeda)

I was strongly attracted to this earthenware vase, entitled "Napoleon's Hat," when I saw it at an exhibit. I used belvedere here as an extension of the vase itself, capped by the red anthurium, expressing Napoleon's glorious achievements, and the berries, as his medals.

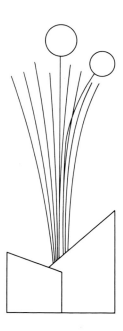

Dedicated to Chagall

MATERIALS: Sweet Pea, Gloriosa, White Lace Flower
CONTAINER: Gray vase with two openings

The flowers seem ready to fly up into the air. Chagall's use of color has always impressed me, and I love to bring his colors into my arrangements.

I don't know how many times I visited Chagall's house perched on a hill in southern France. His gentle smile always welcomed me, and he called me "Madame Energetic"! I will never forget his words: "Nature is our teacher."

NOTE: Queen Anne's lace can be an excellent substitution for white lace flower.

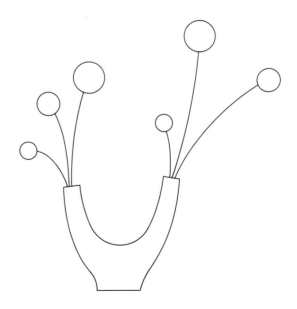

Queen Fabiola

MATERIALS: Anthurium, Anemone, dried tree root, Willow
CONTAINER: Made by the author (Majorca)

The purple anemones appear to be wrapped up by the tree roots, while the willow reaches out from the soft blue container. This arrangement is my image of the gentle queen, whose warmth overflows into the fairy tales she writes for children.

I gave a demonstration of a flower arrangement when I was invited to Europalia Japan '89 in Belgium. At that time, I was invited to the palace, and presented this arrangement to the queen. The tea party I enjoyed there remains a wonderful memory.

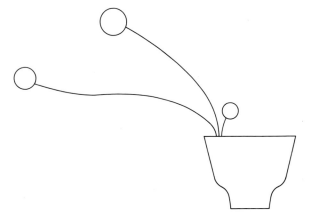

A Song for Mother

MATERIALS: Carnation, Pine
CONTAINER: Made by the author

Carnations, traditional Mother's-Day flowers, look out
from three points, lovingly sheltered by pine branches. I
used these gentle colors to express my feelings for my late
mother in this dedication to her.

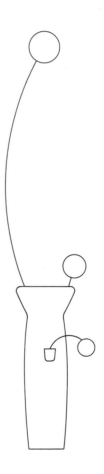

Bolshoi Circus

MATERIALS: Showy Lily (White), Indian Ginger Lily
CONTAINER: Made by the author (Majorca)

I can still vividly recall the Bolshoi Circus from my trip to
Moscow. As I made this arrangement, I tried to capture
the wonders of circus life.

Although containers are usually static and sedentary by
their nature, I gave this pot a sense of movement by ad-
ding an undulation to the clay. The entire arrangement
appears to be ready to dance across a stage or take a trip
on the flying trapeze.

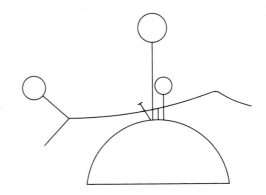

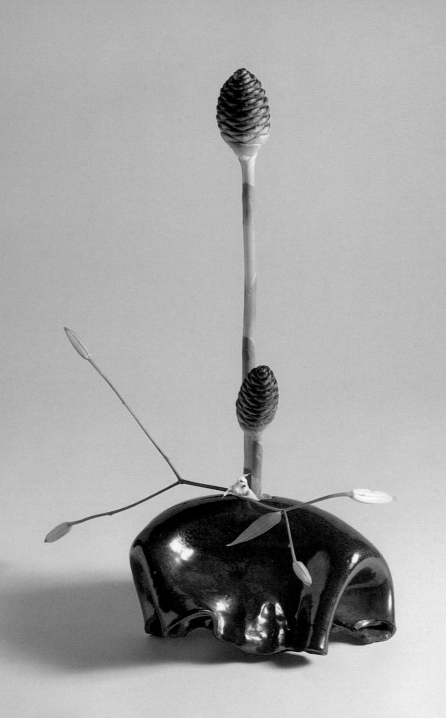

South Pacific

MATERIALS: Leucadendron, Sea Fan, Mulberry
CONTAINER: Earthenware (Italy)

I was surprised to discover that the sea off New Zealand has a different color from the sea in Japan. The dried seaweed expresses my image of the Pacific Ocean in the southern hemisphere, and the curved mulberry branch suggests the waves.

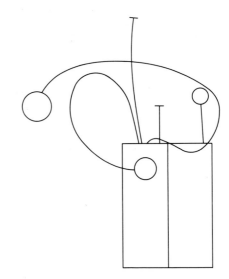

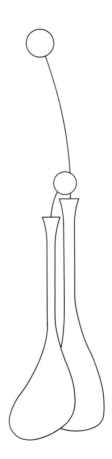

Lovers

MATERIALS: Scarlet Kaffir Lily
CONTAINER: Glassware (Vienna)

The scarlet kaffir lilies in the beautiful two-part Viennese glassware seem to lean in towards each other like two lovers sharing a secret.

Polka Dance

MATERIALS: Sweet Scabious, Camellia
CONTAINER: Designed by the author

A bright and lively folk dance. You can almost hear the polka music in the background. This arrangement is simplicity itself, but there is a fine balance between the lines and colors.

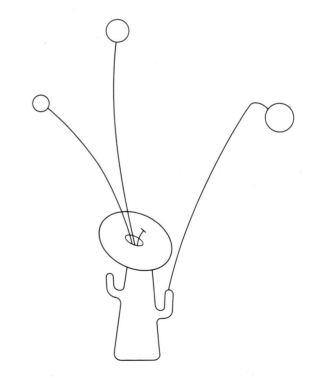

Merlion

MATERIALS: Wild Plantain, Chinese Peach branch (dried)
CONTAINER: Earthenware (Singapore)

Whenever I arrive in Singapore, the white Merlion—symbol of Singapore—is there to greet me. I made this arrangement entirely from local materials to express an image of this mythical sea-dwelling lion.

Memories

MATERIALS: Pomegranate, Variegated Pine, *Buckleya lanceolata*
CONTAINER: Made by the author (Majorca)

This arrangement uses Japanese materials but a modern, western-style setting. Birds soaring against the high Majorcan sky are expressed by the lovely blossoms.

The containers I made in Majorca in 1984 are still a big part of the arrangements I create today, as you can see from the many arrangements in this book that use Majorca-made containers. This container, which bears my signature on one side, is made to represent the island of Majorca. My memories of those days will live with me forever.

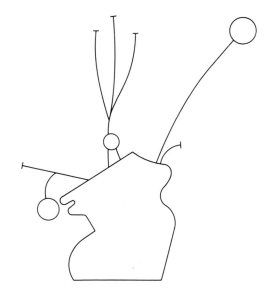

BASIC INSTRUCTIONS FOR STUDENTS OF IKEBANA

FUNDAMENTAL METHODS AND STYLES

Ikebana arrangements are created using certain basic methods and styles. The *moribana* ("piling flowers") method uses relatively low containers and *kenzan,* or needle point holders, to support the flowers in their positions, whereas *nageire* ("tossed in")-method arrangements use high containers or vases and no *kenzan.* Both methods require three chief branch groups of flowers, and the relative position of these groups results in one of four primary styles: upright, slanting, horizontal, or hanging. In addition, although the first and second chief branch groups always face left in a natural arrangement, these branches may be arranged to face right, which is called a reverse arrangement.

Chief branches

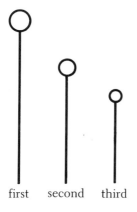

first   second   third

Three Branch Groups

Basic arrangements in both *moribana* and *nageire* methods always contain three chief branches or stalks. A branch group may be a single flower, a group of flowers on the same stem, a leaf, or a tree branch with both flowers and leaves. The first branch group is the longest, the second is shorter, and the third is shortest. Besides these three, any number of subsidiary branches may be used to supplement one of the chief branch groups.

Length of the Branch Groups

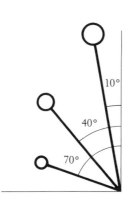

The length of each chief branch depends on the environment in which the arrangement is to be placed and on the materials used in the arrangement; it also must be in proportion with the width (A) and the depth (B) of the container to be used. If you want to make a spectacularly large arrangement, the length of the first branch should be 2 x (A + B). In a medium-sized arrangement, the length of the first branch should be 1-1/2 x (A + B). If you want to make your arrangement comparatively small, the length of the first branch should be (A + B).

The length of the remaining two branch groups is determined by the first chief branch. The second branch should be 3/4 the length of the first, and the third should be 1/2 the length of the second. Subsidiary branches are usually shorter than the chief branches.

The Four Basic Styles

Both *moribana* and *nageire* arrangements can be made using upright, slanting, horizontal, and hanging styles, which are produced by varying the angles of the three chief branch groups, depending on the types of materials used and the impression the arranger wants to convey. In a given style *moribana* and *nageire* arrangements use the same angles for the chief branches.

The upright style is characterized by a stationary, steady mood. The accent is always on the first chief branch, reaching straight up into the heavens. Supporting branches in upright-style arrangements are mainly used to supplement one of the chief branches or, in *moribana*, to cover the *kenzan*.

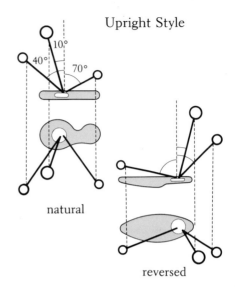

Upright Style

natural

reversed

Upright Style

1

2

3

Slanting Style

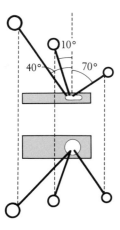

The slanting style is more rhythmical than the upright style. For the angled branch groups, be sure to insert the stems in the *kenzan* in an upright position first, and then adjust them to the reclining position.

Horizontal-style arrangements are best viewed from above. Floating flowers and glass containers work especially well in this kind of arrangement, but take care that no *kenzan* are visible from any angle. Either use no *kenzan* at all, or keep it well hidden with pebbles, sand, or subsidiary branches.

The hanging style is used to show off the beauty of materials such as willow branches, eucalyptus, and vines. Hanging-style arrangements, as the name implies, may be hung on a wall—traditionally, hanging-style arrangements are hung in Japanese *tokonoma* alcoves—or placed on a shelf where they can be viewed from above or below.

Slanting Style

1

2

3

Horizontal Style

1

2

Horizontal Style

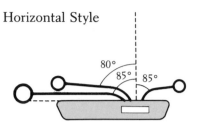

Hanging Style

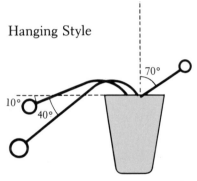

For an example of a hanging-style arrangement, please see p. 39.

Variations

There are infinite possibilities for variations on the four basic styles. The key is to follow your your instincts in harmony with the flowers and materials. Some of the variations I have had success with are: the divided style, which arranges the chief branches in two separate *kenzan* placed apart in the container, yielding a sense of space; floating flower arrangements (see facing page); and the duet style, where baby's breath or other materials are placed near each principal branch to form duets. Also, *moribana* and *nageire* arrangements can be displayed together in a combination of containers. Sometimes the containers themselves will suggest new variations—by having more than one opening, for example. The *morimono* style, a combination of flowers and fruits, is another possibility. As your joy in creating arrangements increases and your understanding of the flowers deepens, you will be able to come up with endless variations of your own.

Floating Flowers

In a floating flower arrangement, the water itself must be arranged with as much care as the flowers are. If possible, use no *kenzan* at all. If you must use *kenzan*, use a smaller one and cover it well with pebbles or other materials. Glassware or natural materials such as sea shells work best as containers. Place the arrangement so that it can be viewed from above.

Container with two openings

Floating flower arrangement

Pruning Shears

At the hardware shop, ask for the "warabite"-type shears, and be sure to try several in order to find those which seem right for your hand. The scissors will be difficult to use if they are too stiff or too loose. With some practice you can easily get used to handling the shears. Rub oil on your shears from time to time and they will last longer.

Warabite shears

Kenzan (Needle Point Holders)

The most common *kenzan* are round or crescent-shaped. They may be used together or separately. If you want to use big materials, you should use rectangular ones for steadiness. Extremely small *kenzan* are now increasingly used for arrangements using glasses, glassware, and miniature vessels as containers. If your *kenzan* is not as steady as you hoped, place small pebbles around it and on top of it to give it a helping hand. When silver objects are used as containers, place silver foil under the *kenzan* for protection. If *kenzan* are unavailable, use several stones the size of your fist or smaller to support the materials.

Kenzan

Water Spray (Pump)

You can make your ikebana all the more vivid and lively by the use of a water spray—especially in hot, sultry summer weather. By reversing the bugle-shaped head part, you can turn a water spray into a water pump which can force water into the stems of such aquatic plants as lotuses, water-lilies, candocks, and others.

Water spray

Saws

Although a pair of pruning shears will do in most cases, you should have a small saw handy for the purpose of cutting hard branches.

Needle-Repairer

Kenzan needles are liable to bend. The needle-repairer straightens the needles effortlessly.

Wire

Wire can be used to tie materials together, and, if made into a rough ball, wire can become an excellent substitute for *kenzan*, especially in small vessels such as glasses.

Pebbles and Sand (Black and White)

By covering the *kenzan* with small pebbles you can make your arrangements all the more natural and beautiful. Use white pebbles in black containers and vice versa for contrast. In some cases sand may be used.

Water-Change Pump

Use a syphon-type rubber pump to change water in the containers.

Preservation Liquids (Chemicals)

In order to prevent decay, administer certain chemicals, such as alcohol, acetic acid, peppermint oil, and others, to the cut part of the stems of materials. Salt is also very good for decay prevention.

Saws

Needle-repairer

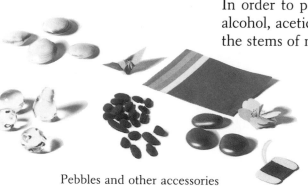

Pebbles and other accessories

Water-change pump

MATERIALS

Flowers and Branches

Most ikebana arrangements are combinations of flowers, branches, and leaves, but anything that fits the image you have in mind and matches the setting will do. Generally, you should combine two or more types of plants in a single arrangement. You can, however, create lovely effects with single species such as camellias, daffodils, cherry boughs, irises, sweet flags, clematis, cosmos, or roses of one color. Select forms and colors that harmonize, and your sense of beauty will work magic in blending and contrasting shape and shape, color and color, line and line.

Dried Materials

In addition to the many variations of everlastings, wood roses, and other dried materials commercially available, your autumn and winter arrangements will take on a new flair if you go into the woods and fields and gather armfuls of berries and grasses yourself, bring them home, dry them, and use them alone or in combination with other materials. Arrangements of dried materials have a distinctive beauty and elegance that people all over the world appreciate.

Other Natural Materials

Combinations of vegetables, vines, fruits, roots, driftwood, pieces of logs, gourds, pumpkins, berries, and many more natural materials of all shapes and colors make appealing arrangements and table centerpieces.

Artificial Materials

Modern ikebana artists have begun to incorporate artificial materials in their arrangements in combination with natural materials. Also, for show windows or exhibitions, it is sometimes necessary to use materials that last longer than natural flowers and branches.

Plastics, steel wire, and glass are often effective, but it takes practice to make artificial materials as emotionally satisfying as natural ones. For long-lasting displays, try dried, bleached, or otherwise processed natural materials first.

Water

A sense of coolness in your flower arrangement can be delightfully refreshing. Try to use the least possible amount of materials, leaving at least two-thirds of the water surface free of flowers. Frequent changes of water in the container preserves flowers longer and keeps the water looking clean. In hot weather, try putting some ice cubes into the water. Also, when you spray water onto the leaves, take care not to wet the flowers.

CONTAINERS

What exactly are most beautiful containers? That is a question I am not bold enough to answer. In the art of flower arrangements, containers do not exist by themselves but only in combination with the flowers and other materials. Always select the containers in full consideration of the flowers you are going to use so that the two will create perfect harmony in color, shape, and all respects. Containers should also complement the surroundings in which the arrangements are to be placed.

Containers are roughly divided into two major categories—those which are created from the start as vases for flower arrangements and those which are borrowed impromptu for the purpose. Possible containers are everywhere—fruit baskets, straw hats, ordinary bottles, jugs, cut glassware, and many others. Bamboo tubes can also make excellent containers if handled correctly.

The safest colors for containers are black and white, while the simplest in form go quite well with almost all kinds of materials. Avoid containers that have elaborate designs as they are liable to

clash with the images you are trying to create with the flowers. Try to find potential flower containers around you and develop your sense of beauty by using them as much as possible. Folk-art wares made for practical purposes can also make interesting vehicles for your arrangements. By using these and other objects, you can create unexpectedly beautiful arrangements which ordinary flower containers cannot support.

In 1984, I went to Majorca to participate in a pottery workshop. Each of the vases I made there—sixty in all—has a special meaning for me. You, too, may find that making vases yourself adds a new dimension to your arrangements, bringing them that much closer to the concept of ikebana as total art.

Always remember that successful arrangements are the result of the harmonious combination of the materials, the containers, and your own lifestyle and environment.

TRIMMING TECHNIQUES

Skill with the Scissors

Slip the top handle of the scissors over your thumb, and rest it well down at the base of your thumb. The bottom handle should rest in the bend of your other four fingers. The cutting action comes from firmly and steadily closing your entire hand, not your fingertips alone. Though some people put their index finger in the handle to cut, this in fact only reduces the power of your cut. The quickest way to master good cutting techniques is to think of hanging the scissors on your thumb and using the rest of your hand to do the work.

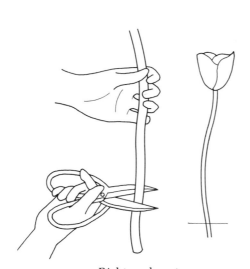

Right-angle cut

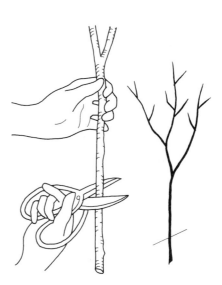

Diagonal cut

Flowers

Though in nature a haphazard profusion of flowers is delightful, for arrangements we must select just those flowers which create the mood or effect we want. First, clip away all withered or crushed blossoms; next, carefully examine the material, and trim away everything but the flowers you know will contribute to the desired effect.

If you are going to use a *kenzan,* you will have to cut fleshy stem plants at right angles. Cutting them on a diagonal increases the area of the opening and correspondingly the ability of the stalk to take in water. This is desirable if your arrangement is one for a deep vase in which you will not require a *kenzan,* but if you do use one, the diagonal cut results in a fragile end that splits on the *kenzan* points.

Do not chop flower stems. Give them a clean cut.

Cut fleshy stems at right angles when using a *kenzan.*

Branches

Trimming branches enlivens by abbreviating and improving the natural materials. Do not be timid. Clip away unwanted branches with a bold hand, and your arrangements are sure to be much lovelier. Cut at forks only, because cutting a branch midway leaves unsightly scars and debris. If you must leave a scar in a branch either by cutting away a large leaf or by cutting midway, hide it by tinting the opening with India ink.

Cut branches on an angle to increase water intake.

Leaves

Cut leaves to accent strengths in the lines and the colors. Select the ones you will leave on the branch with a careful eye to the beauty of the individual plant's characteristics. Be sure to use only the leaves that will play a vital part in your arrangement. In ikebana there is no room for non-essentials.

Leaves can be manipulated in various ways to give your arrangements a sense of movement. Roll the tips of wide leaves with your fingers for gentle curl, and pass the tops of slender leaves through a slit in the center vein for an interesting ribbon-like effect.

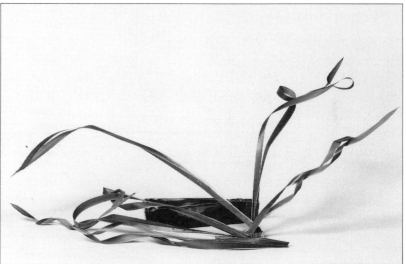

Basic Method

Keeping your elbows close to your body, apply pressure with your thumbs to the point you want to bend. If the material is a fleshy grass-like plant, crush it slightly beforehand at the bending point. Crushing will not damage the tough, water-transporting fibers of even the most delicate plants.

Slitting and Bending

Some thick woody stalks and branches offer so much resistance that it is difficult to bend them using the basic method, but reckless use of the knife weakens them and makes them easy to break. Slitting the point you want to bend will enable you to shape the branch properly.

Wedging and Bending

In branches too tough even for the slit method, make a cut from the outside with a saw. The depth will vary with the texture of the wood, but in most cases a cut about two-thirds of the diameter of the branch will suffice. After making the cut, find another branch of about the same thickness as the one you are working with, and, using your saw, cut from it a V-shaped wedge thick enough to achieve the desired bend and deep enough to fill the slit in the first branch.

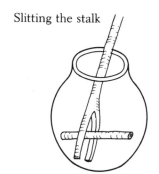

Slitting the stalk

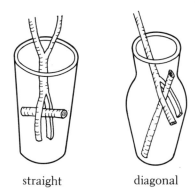

straight   diagonal

FIXING MATERIALS IN VASES

Since *nageire* arrangements are made without the use of *kenzan*, many techniques have been developed to help the materials stand in their vases in beautifully natural ways.

Slit the Stalk

For most of the deeper jar- and bottle-shaped vases, cut small pieces of branches in lengths that will fit firmly either straight or diagonally across the inside of the vase. Cut slits in the bottoms of the stems of the floral materials and fit them on the braces in the vase.

No Braces

Place one stalk firmly in the vase and prop all the other flowers against it.

Single-Flower Prop

Fix a single flower in place by propping it against the side of a vase.

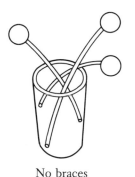

No braces

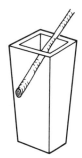

Single-flower prop

Fork Prop

Cut a short stalk, cut a slit in the bottom of the material, fit the two together, and put them into the vase.

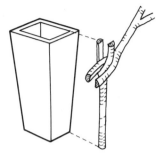

Fork prop

Cross Brace

For wider spacing among the flowers, make a cross brace by tying small bits of stalk together. Slip the cross into the vase, and arrange the materials around it.

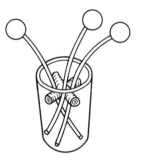

Cross brace

Wire Holder

If the shape of the vase makes *kenzan* or stick braces unsightly or impractical, ball up some fine wire, put it in the bottom of the vase, and fix the materials in it.

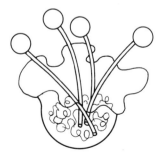

Wire holder

Applications

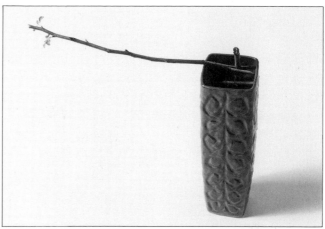

To arrange branches horizontally in tall containers (see p. 98), use the slit-stalk method, with a supporting branch slightly longer than the vase.

Place the branches in the vase. Be sure to hide the supporting branch carefully with stalks of leaves or flowers.

Hollow stems like this amaryllis require a short branch to support them when a kenzan is used.

Cut the supporting stalk slightly longer than the stem of the amaryllis, position it in the kenzan, and slip the amaryllis over the stalk.

FLOWER PRESERVATION METHODS

Cutting Method

Place the stems of the materials in a bucket or a deep bowl filled with fresh water. With your shears under the water, cut one-inch pieces from the stalks until the materials are the length you want for your arrangement. Leave the materials in the water for about ten minutes after cutting because the water pressure promotes water intake.

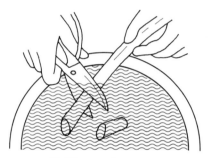

Cutting under water

Flowers Direct from the Garden

Always try to cut flowers from your garden either early in the morning or after sunset. Fill a container with water and take it with you so that you can immediately cut your flowers under water and let them stand for a good drink. Be sure you do this with flowers such as morning glories and hydrangeas. Sprinkle a pinch of salt around camellia stamens, and spray the blossom with a fine mist. The salt will cause the pollen to rise and prevent the blossom from shedding its petals. If a particularly lovely camellia blossom falls off, carefully fix the petals in place with a toothpick.

Flowers Needing Extra Water

Plant materials that have been kept out of water for a long time, such as flowers gathered on a trip to the country, should be given a chance to take in water before they are cut. Dip the materials in cold water, wrap them in newspaper, moisten the paper, and lay the flowers on their sides for about thirty minutes in a place protected from sunlight and wind.

Charring

Wrap flowers in paper and quickly char the cut ends of the stems over a gas flame, alcohol lamp, or candle. Dip the ends in cold water immediately. Carbonizing the ends stimulates the plant and prevents bacteria growth.

Hot-Water Treatment

Wrap the blossoms and upper parts of the material in paper as for charring, above, and dip the cut ends in hot water. This method is effective for tender, soft materials that would be damaged by the charring method.

Cutting and Crushing

Making horizontal and vertical cuts in the ends of materials or crushing the ends with scissors will improve their ability to take in water.

Chemical Application

After cutting the materials in water, rub chemicals such as salt, baking soda, burnt alum, etc., to the cut ends of the stems. You can also dissolve these chemicals in the water of the flower vase. This method is effective for all kinds of plants. Salt is especially effective on plants such as Chinese bell flowers and garbella.

Chemical Treatment

This method is used to sterilize flowers. Place the materials in diluted alcohol, acetic acid, peppermint oil, or ammonia for ten to twenty minutes after cutting them. Be careful not to make the solution too strong or the plants will wither. A couple of drops of apple vinegar in the water of the vase is also very effective. Acetic acid is good for plants such as pampas grass and millet, while alcohol is best for wisteria and other vines.

Water Pumping

To give lotuses and water lilies the extra water they require, prepare a solution of tobacco water by wrapping cigarette ends in cloth and soaking them in water, or a tea solution by boiling tea until it is quite strong. Using your water pump, fill the stalks of the leaves and the blossoms with one of these solutions, and seal the cut end with alum. This will help fresh and healthy materials last longer.

Water pumping

A LIFE WITH FLOWERS

Born in 1920, Noriko Ohno began her studies of formal ikebana in 1937 after high school graduation. She studied classical and formal arrangements through the Ikenobo Ryuseiha school and learned the basics of modern *moribana* and *nageire* from the Sogetsu school. Her dream of multinational, multicultural ikebana began to take form while she was holding classes in flower arrangement for non-Japanese students at the American Club in Tokyo, and, beginning in 1954 with her work as a cultural envoy, she soon became very active on the international scene, traveling from continent to continent to give ikebana demonstrations and exhibitions at the invitation of public and private organizations. What follows is a chronology of her major achievements in almost a half century of commitment to the world of ikebana.

1954–55: Selected to participate in San Paulo's Quatercentennial; spent one full year giving floral demonstrations throughout the cities of North and South America, Europe, Scandinavia, the Middle East, and Southeast Asia as a cultural envoy; the ikebana exhibition she held by invitation of the French government was the first of its kind to be held in Paris. Founded the Kokusai Ikebana Association upon her return to Japan in April 1955.

1958: Represented the Japanese government at the Brussels World's Fair.

1961: Invited to participate in Switzerland's International Modern Design Exhibition.

1963: Demonstrations at the Musee Guimet and in many European countries; demonstration at Hawaii's East-West Culture Center; donated a glass art relief, "Flowers Are Living," to San Paulo's Japanese Center; interviewed celebrities around the world for *Josei Jishin* magazine, creating ikebana arrangements for each one.

1964: Inaugurated the Monthly Charity Show. One hundred fifty embassies have sponsored these shows in the past twenty-six years.

1966: Demonstrations at the Musee Guimet, Instituto Italiano, and the Cologne Japan Culture Center in West Germany.

1967: Interviewed successful women around the world for *Fujin Koron* magazine, presenting each with an ikebana portrait.

1968: Honorary guest of Yugoslavia; served as a judge for the first Monte Carlo Flora competition; charity show at Tokyo's Kabukiza theater.

1973: Constructed the "Castle of Flowers" school for the Kokusai Ikebana Association in the Aoyama district of Tokyo.

1974: Demonstration in Switzerland on invitation of Japan-Swiss Association.

1975: Sponsored by the Japan Foundation on a visit to Brazil, where she was awarded the Brazilian government's Cultural Medal; demonstrations in Paraguay, Peru, and the United States (Pasadena).

1977: Presented the Japan Red Cross with flowers at its opening ceremony; visited Czechoslovakia and Hungary with the sponsorship of the Japan Foundation; presented Malaysia's Prime Minister with a floral arrangement celebrating his visit to Japan.

1978: Participated in Charity Show in Singapore; ikebana demonstration at East Germany's Trade Center opening.

1979: Demonstrations throughout Italy; awarded Gold Medal of Friendship.

1980: Demonstrations in Tunisia, Belgium, and France.

1981: Floral trip to Kokusai Ikebana chapters in Malaysia, Singapore, and Taipei; invited to Bulgaria's 1300th anniversary celebration; demonstration at EC Hall in Belgium for its Foreign Ministry.

1982: 1000th demonstration held abroad.

1983: Demonstrations in Paris, Denmark, and the Netherlands; awarded a Gold Medal by Singapore's Red Cross.

1984: Floral exhibition in Majorca, Spain; attended Japan-USSR Roundtable Conference; demonstrations in Moscow, Tallinn, and Leningrad.

1985: Demonstrations in Malaysia, Singapore, and Taipei; demonstrations throughout Brazil, sponsored by the Japan Foundation.

1986: Demonstrations in Singapore, Malta, Assisi (World Wildlife Fund 25th anniversary), Belgium, Poland, Bulgaria, and Austria.

1987: Floral trips to Malaysia and Taipei; Japan Week in New Zealand; demonstration in Australia.

1988: Singapore Community Chest Show; demonstrations in Taiwan, in Malaysia, and at Australia's Bicentennial; attended Japan-USSR Roundtable Conference; demonstrations in Moscow and Tallinn.

1989: Demonstrations in the Baltic states; cultural envoy to Belgium's Europalia Japan 1989; met Queen Fabiola and presented her with "Queen Fabiola," p. 81; demonstrations in Paris and Luxemburg.

1990: Floral trip to Singapore, Hong Kong, and Taiwan; exhibition at the Osaka International Garden and Greenery Exposition.